MW00948093

CORGIS
Coloring Book!

A Unique Collection Of Coloring Pages

Bold Illustrations
COLORING BOOKS

This is a Bleed Through Page If You Are Using a Colouring Marker or Pen!

Find Other Great Titles By searching for Bold Illustrations on Your Favorite Book Retailer

Amazon.Ca | Barnes & Noble (BN.Com) | Books A Million (BAM.Com)

This is a Bleed Through Page If You Are Using a Colouring Marker or Pen!

Find Other Great Titles By searching for Bold Illustrations on Your Favorite Book Retailer

Amazon.Ca | Barnes & Noble (BN.Com) | Books A Million (BAM.Com)

This is a Bleed Through Page If You Are Using a Colouring Marker or Pen!

Find Other Great Titles By searching for Bold Illustrations on Your Favorite Book Retailer

Amazon.Ca | Barnes & Noble (BN.Com) | Books A Million (BAM.Com)

Bold Illustrations

COLORING BOOKS

This is a Bleed Through Page If You Are Using a Colouring Marker or Pen!

Find Other Great Titles By searching for Bold Illustrations on Your Favorite Book Retailer

Amazon.Ca | Barnes & Noble (BN.Com) | Books A Million (BAM.Com)

CPSIA information can be obtained
at www.ICGtesting.com
Printed in the USA
BVHW011032310722
643467BV00016B/166

9 781641 938426